Design 1
For a 4- or 5-sided lampshade.
Suggested lampbase height: 8″.

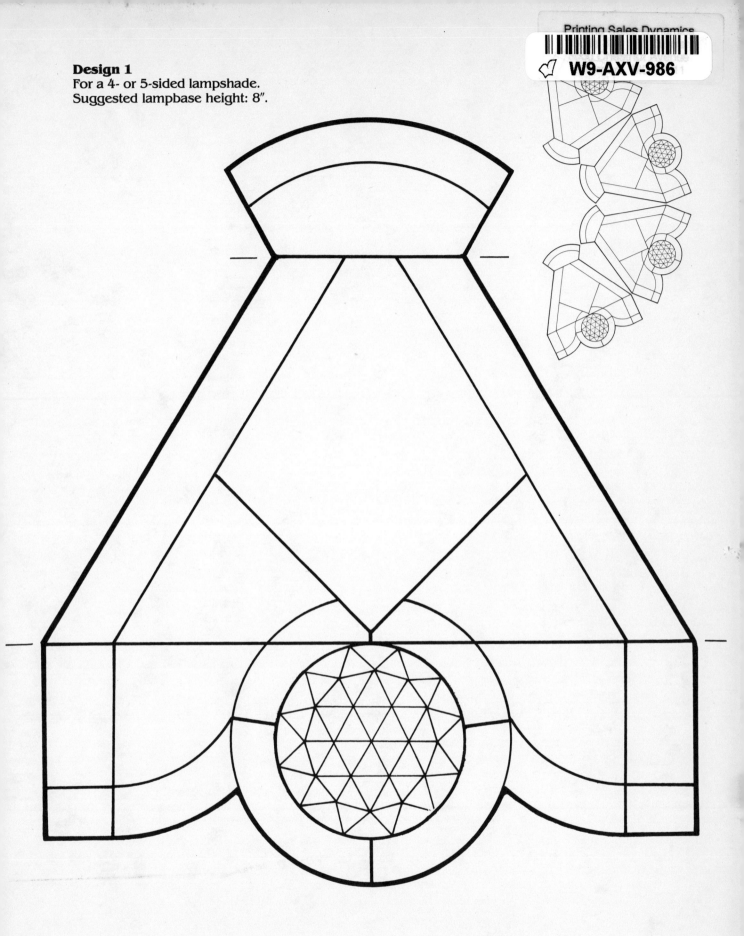

PLATE 1

Design 2
For a 5-sided lampshade.
Suggested lampbase height: 6".

Design 3
For a 4- or 5-sided lampshade.
Suggested lampbase height: 8".

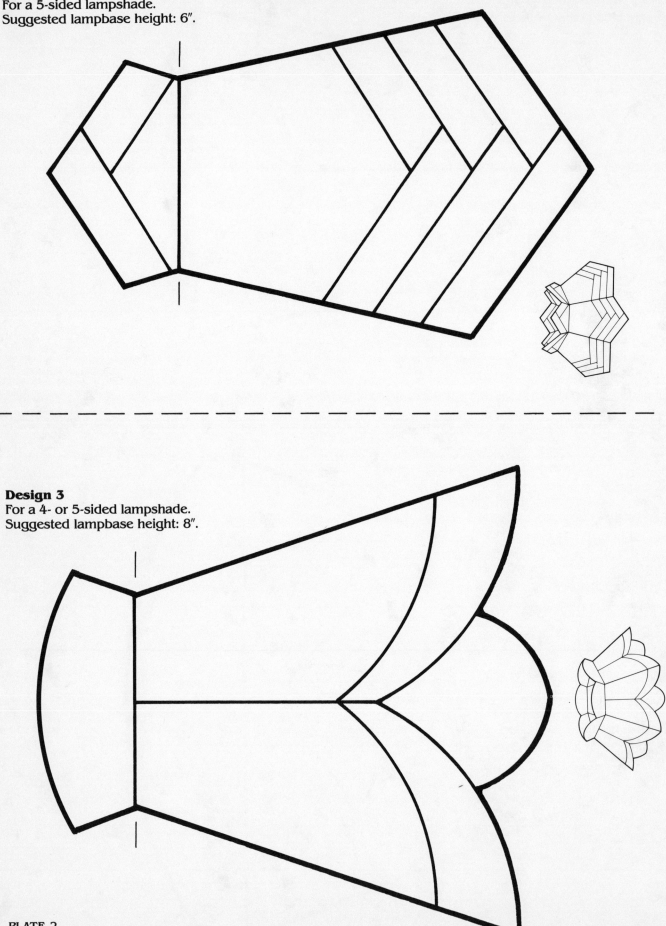

PLATE 2

Design 4
For a 5-sided lampshade.
Suggested lampbase height: 6″.

Design 5
For a 4- or 5-sided lampshade.
Suggested lampbase height: 8″.

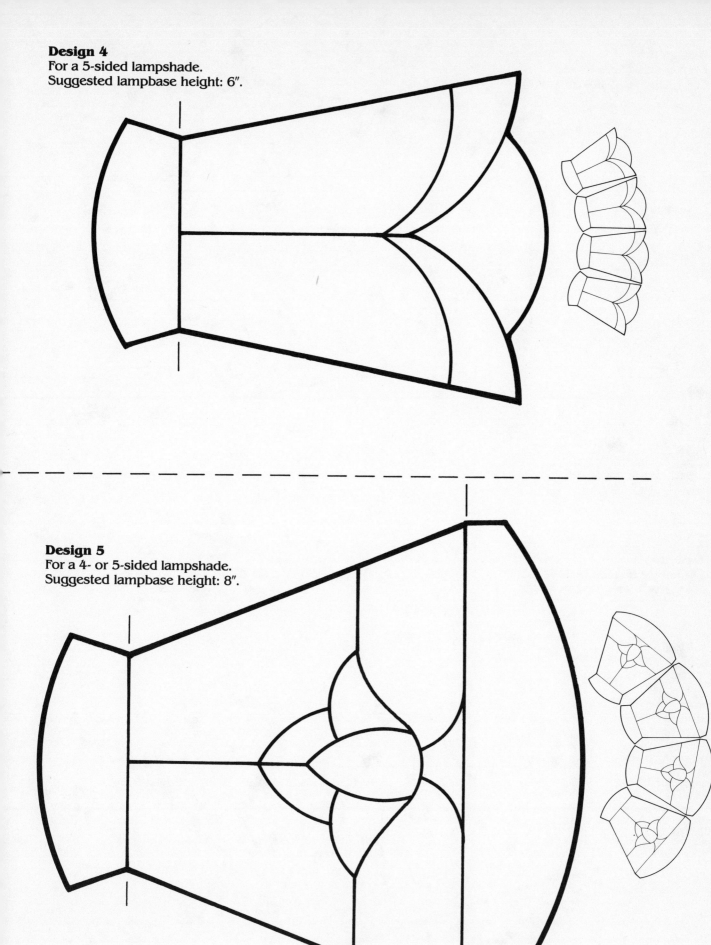

PLATE 3

Design 6
For a 6-sided lampshade.
Suggested lampbase height: 8″.

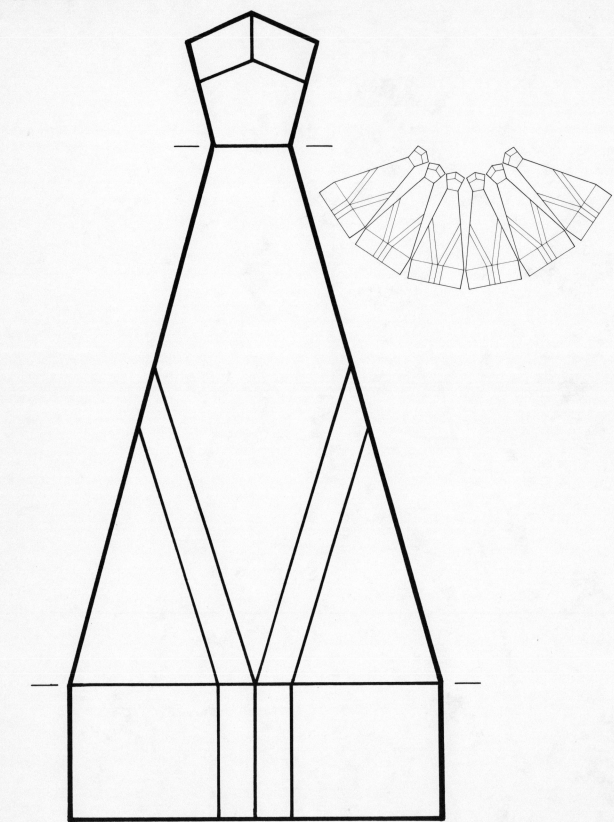

PLATE 4

Design 7
For a 6-sided lampshade.
Suggested lampbase height: 8".

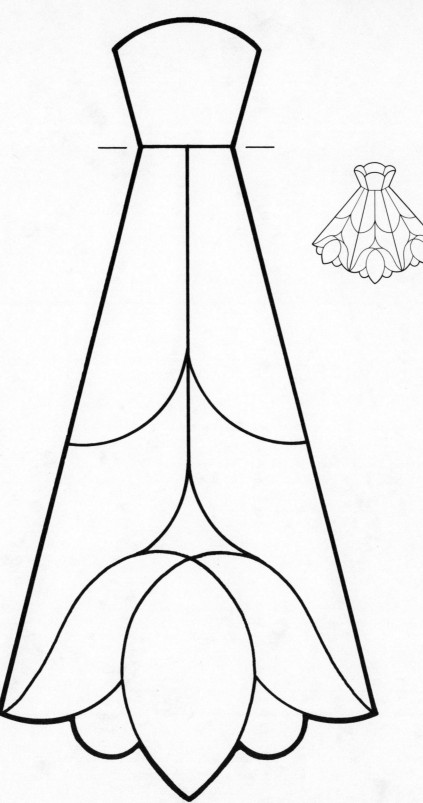

PLATE 5

Design 8
For a 6- or 7-sided lampshade.
Suggested lampbase height: 8".

Design 9
For a 6- or 7-sided lampshade.
Suggested lampbase height: 8".

PLATE 6

Design 10
For a 6- or 7-sided lampshade.
Suggested lampbase height: 8″.

Design 11
For a 6- or 7-sided lampshade.
Suggested lampbase height: 8″.

PLATE 7

Design 12
For a 7-sided lampshade.
Suggested lampbase height: 6″.

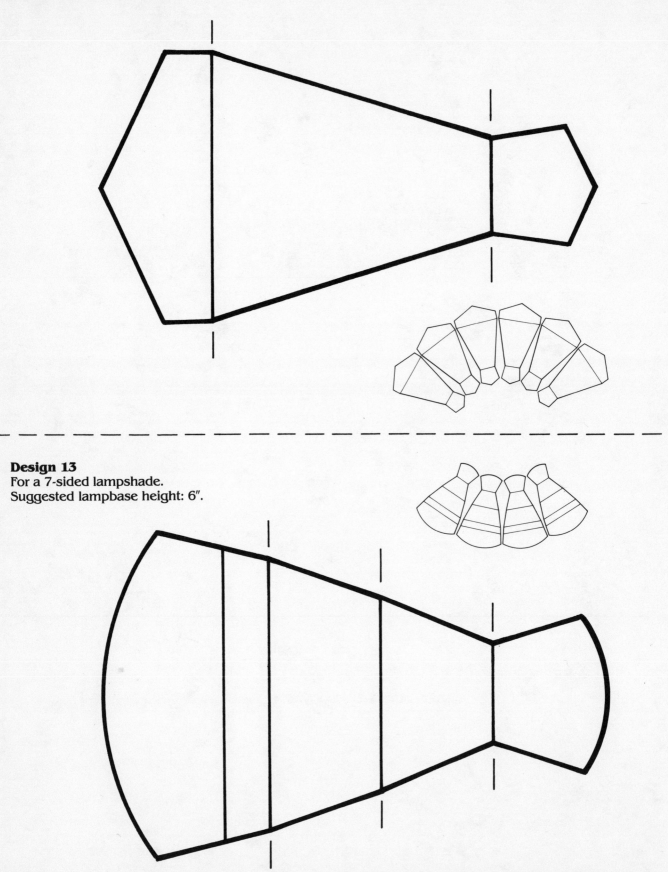

Design 13
For a 7-sided lampshade.
Suggested lampbase height: 6″.

PLATE 8

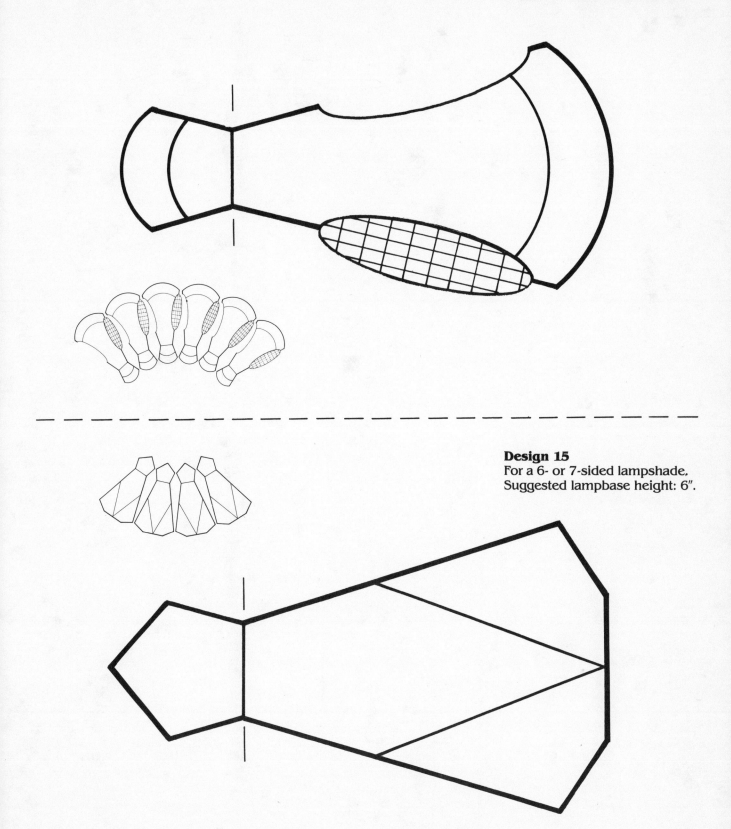

Design 14
For a 6- or 7-sided lampshade.
Suggested lampbase height: 6″.

Design 15
For a 6- or 7-sided lampshade.
Suggested lampbase height: 6″.

PLATE 9

Design 16
For a 14-sided lampshade (make 7 of each panel).
Suggested lampbase height: 8″.

PLATE 10

Design 17
For a 14-sided lampshade (make 7 of each panel).
Suggested lampbase height: 8″.

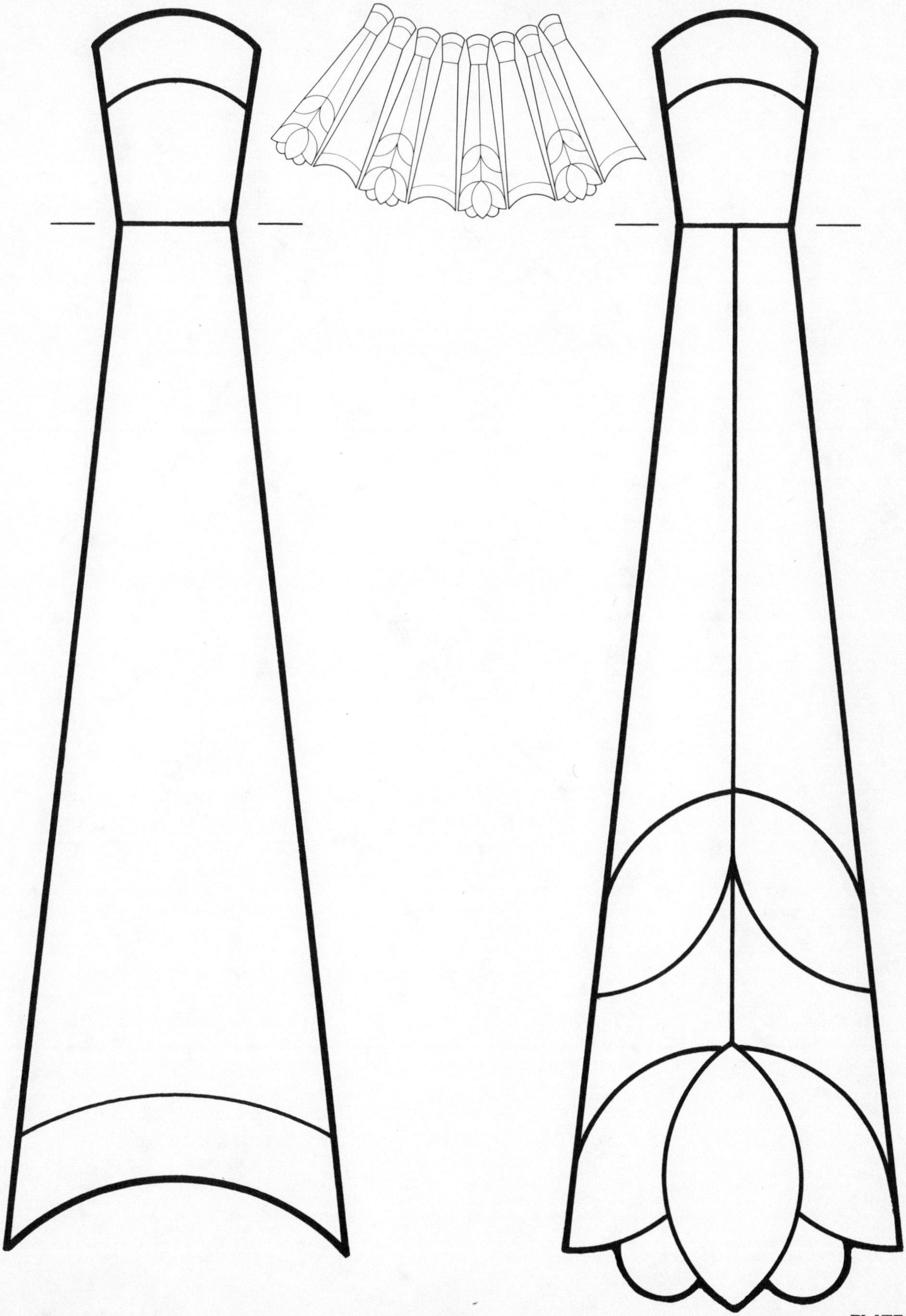

PLATE 11

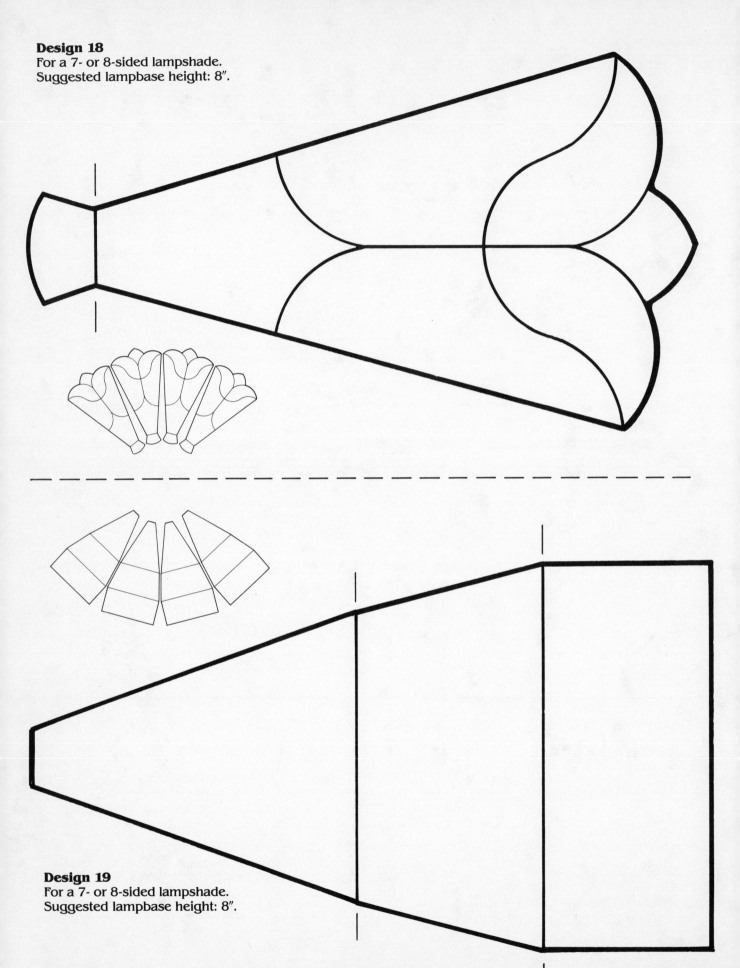

Design 18
For a 7- or 8-sided lampshade.
Suggested lampbase height: 8″.

Design 19
For a 7- or 8-sided lampshade.
Suggested lampbase height: 8″.

PLATE 12

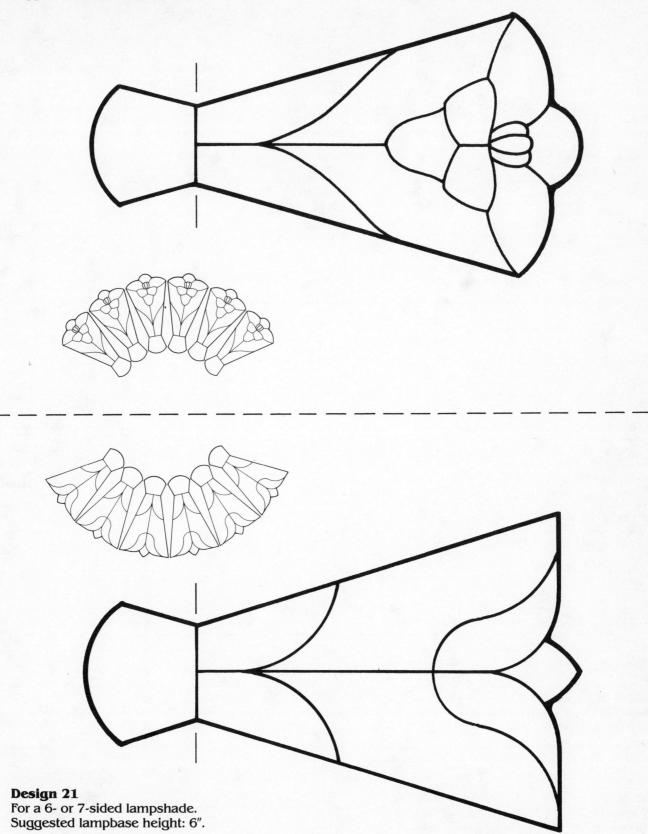

Design 20
For a 6- or 7-sided lampshade.
Suggested lampbase height: 6″.

Design 21
For a 6- or 7-sided lampshade.
Suggested lampbase height: 6″.

PLATE 13

Design 22
For a 4- or 5-sided lampshade.
Suggested lampbase height: 8″ or 9″.

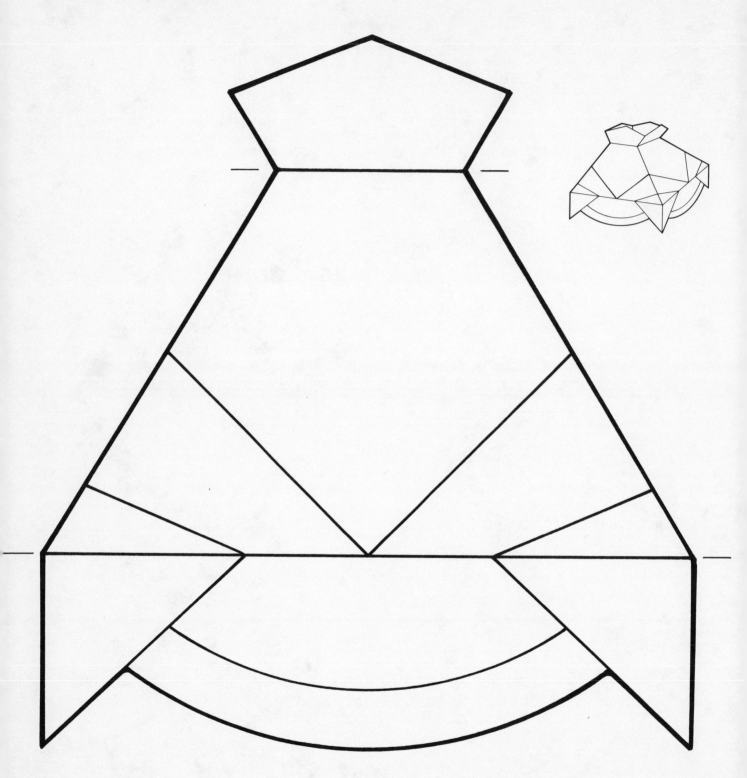

PLATE 14

Design 23
For a 4- or 5-sided lampshade.
Suggested lampbase height: 8″ or 9″.

PLATE 15

Design 24
For a 4- or 5-sided lampshade.
Suggested lampbase height: 6″.

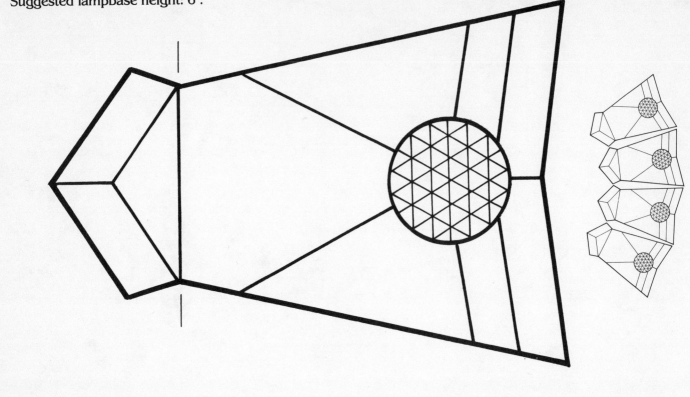

Design 25
For a 5-sided lampshade.
Suggested lampbase height: 8″.

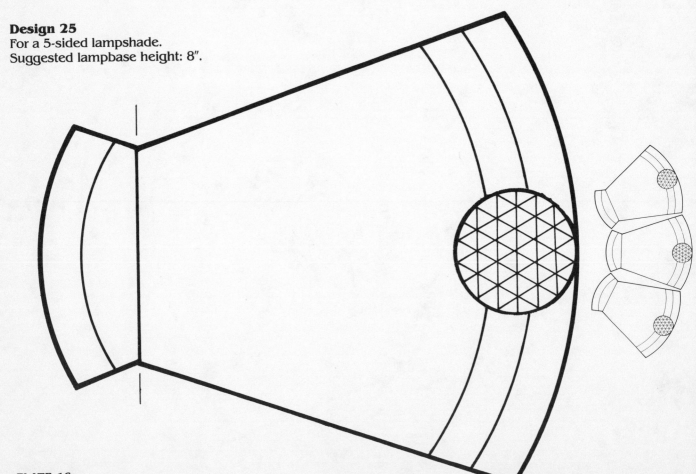

PLATE 16

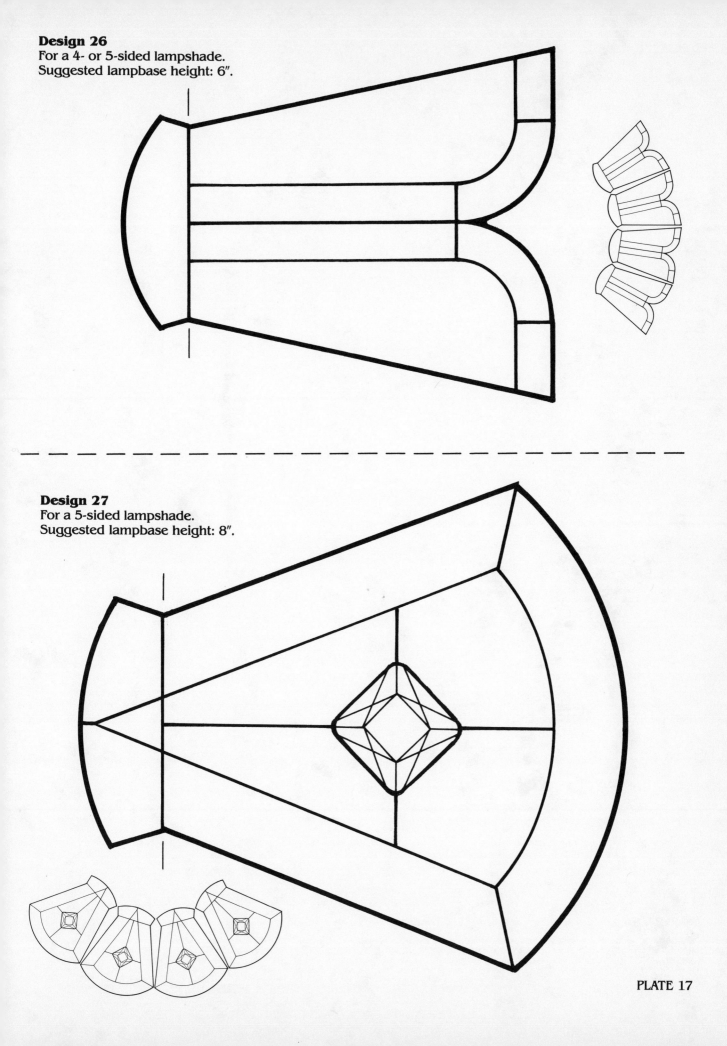

Design 26
For a 4- or 5-sided lampshade.
Suggested lampbase height: 6″.

Design 27
For a 5-sided lampshade.
Suggested lampbase height: 8″.

PLATE 17

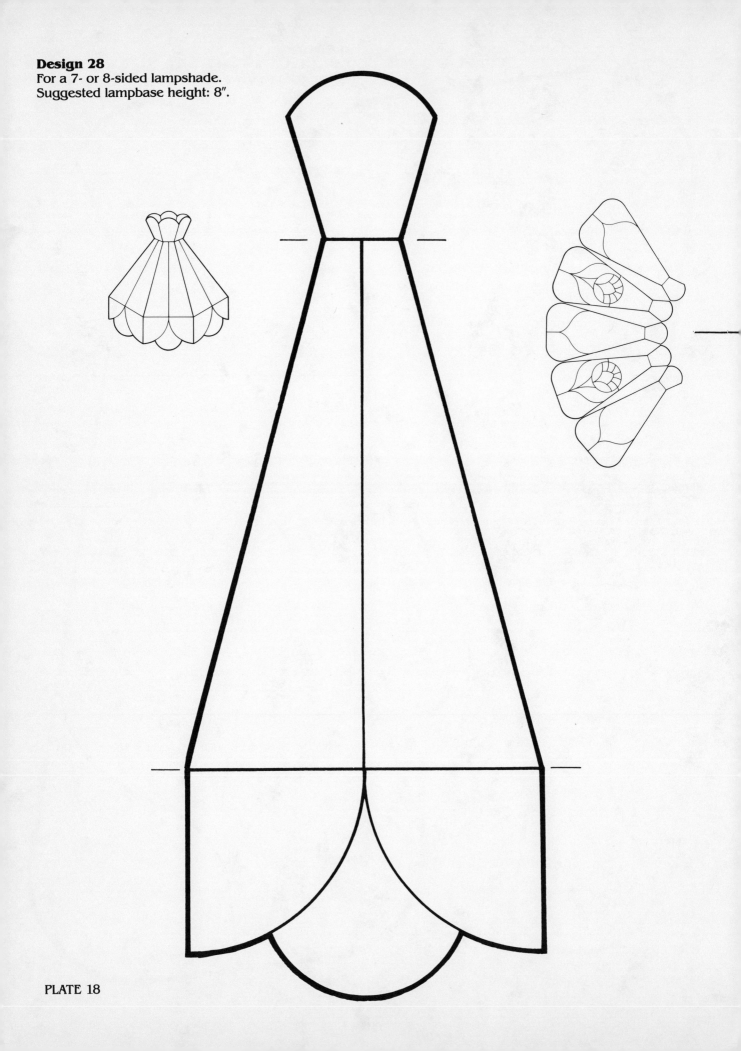

Design 28
For a 7- or 8-sided lampshade.
Suggested lampbase height: 8″.

PLATE 18

Design 29
For a 6-sided lampshade (make 3 of each panel).
Suggested lampbase height: 8".

PLATE 19

Design 30
For a 6-sided lampshade.
Suggested lampbase height: 8″.

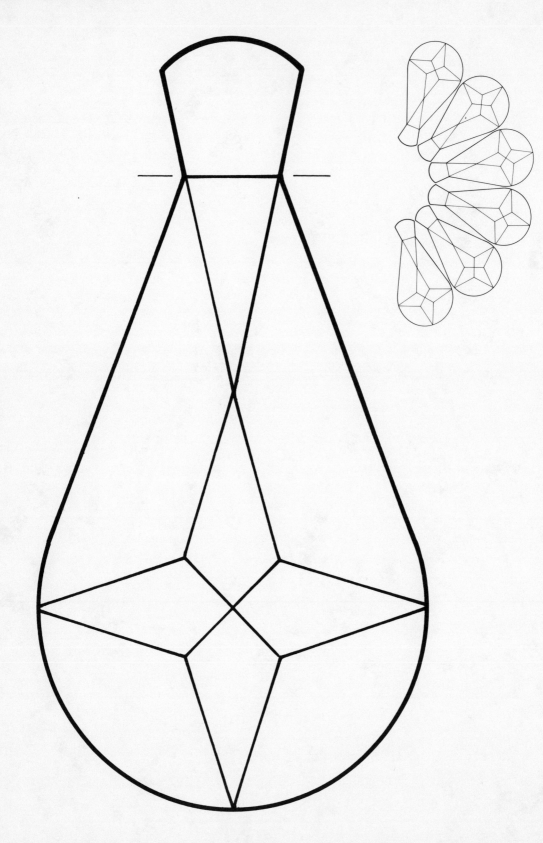

PLATE 20

Design 31
For a 6-sided lampshade.
Suggested lampbase height: 8″.

PLATE 21

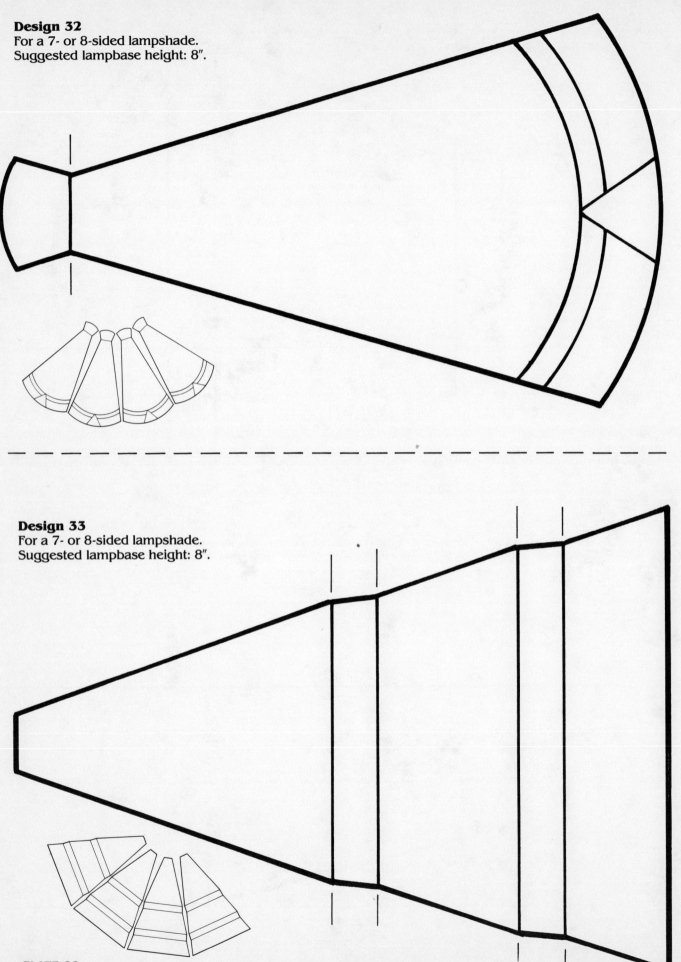

Design 32
For a 7- or 8-sided lampshade.
Suggested lampbase height: 8″.

Design 33
For a 7- or 8-sided lampshade.
Suggested lampbase height: 8″.

PLATE 22

Design 34
For a 4-sided lampshade.
Suggested lampbase height: 6″.

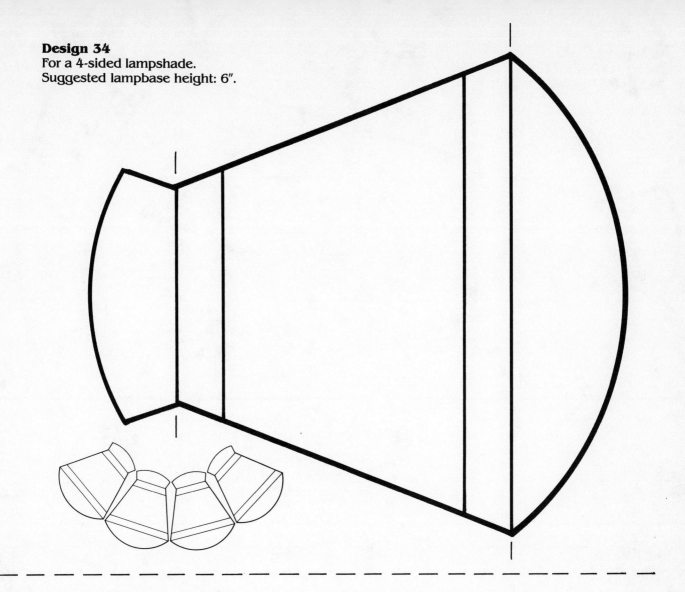

Design 35
For an 8-sided lampshade.
Suggested lampbase height: 6″.

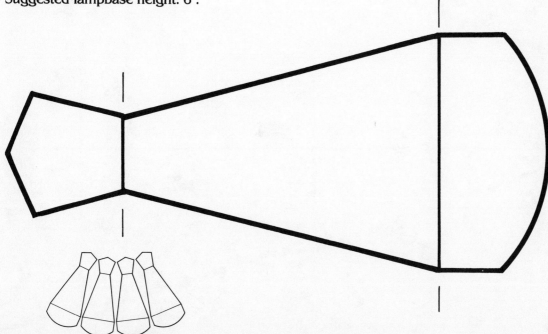

PLATE 23

Design 36
For a 14-sided lampshade (make 7 of each panel).
Suggested lampbase height: 8″.

PLATE 24

Design 37
For a 6-sided lampshade.
Suggested lampbase height: 8".

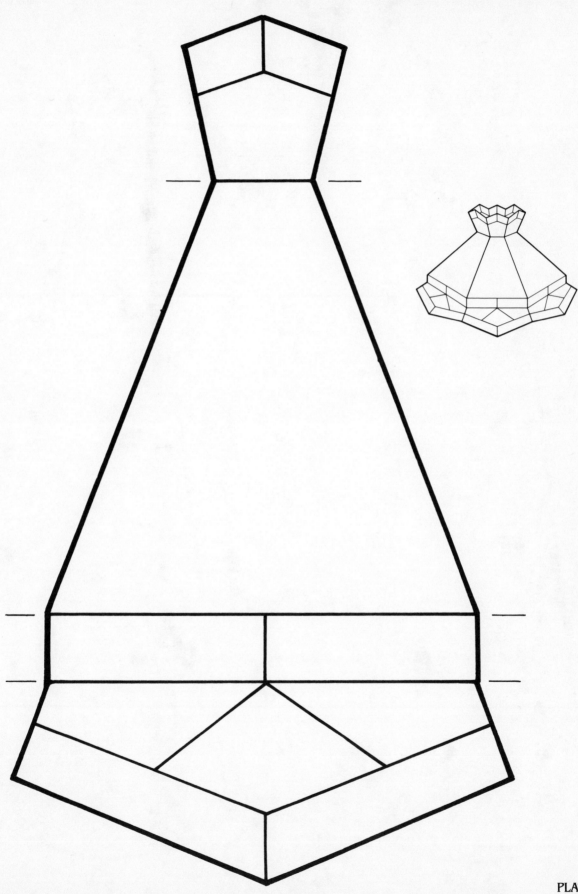

PLATE 25

Design 38
For a 4- or 5-sided lampshade.
Suggested lampbase height: 8″.

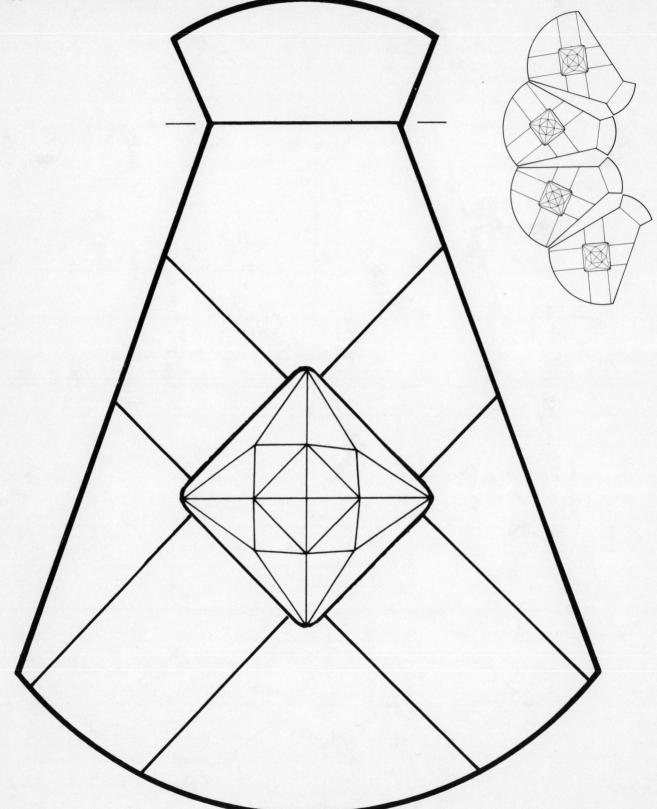

PLATE 26

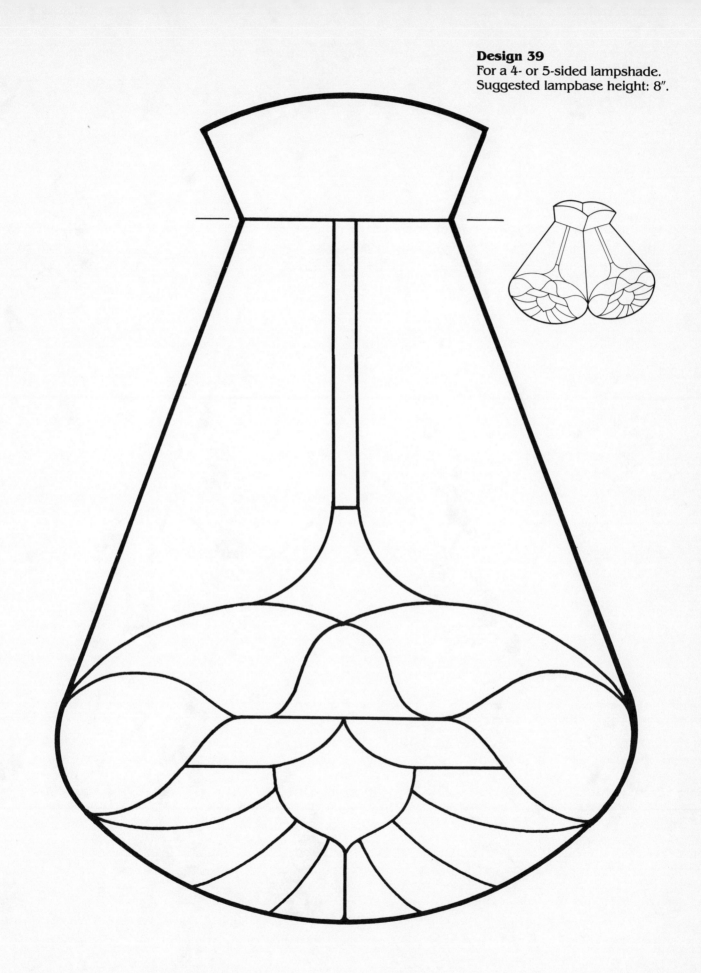

Design 39
For a 4- or 5-sided lampshade.
Suggested lampbase height: 8″.

PLATE 27

Design 40
For a 5-sided lampshade.
Suggested lampbase height: 6″.

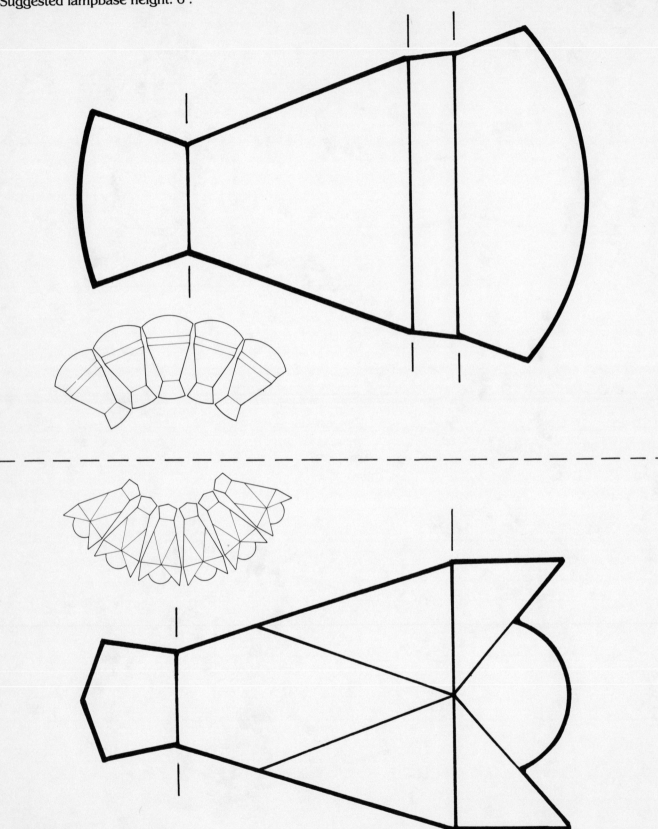

Design 41
For a 6-sided lampshade.
Suggested lampbase height: 6″.

PLATE 28

Design 42
For a 6-sided lampshade.
Suggested lampbase height: 6″.

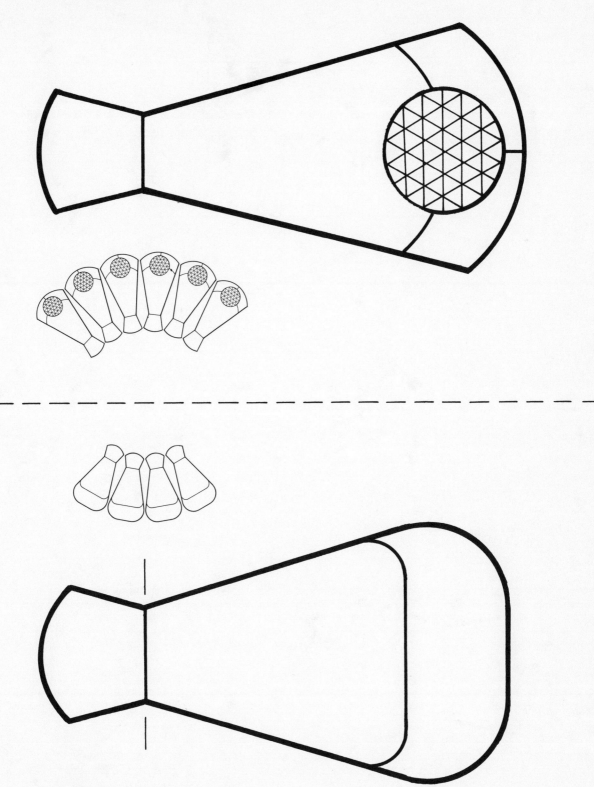

Design 43
For a 6-sided lampshade.
Suggested lampbase height: 6″.

PLATE 29

Design 44
For a 4- or 5-sided lampshade.
Suggested lampbase height: 8″.

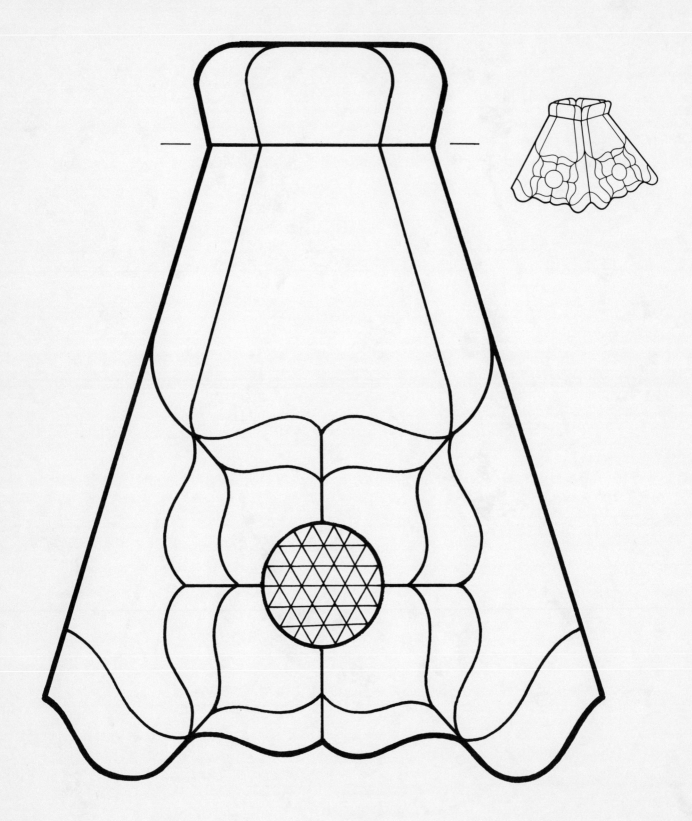

PLATE 30

Design 45
For a 4- or 5-sided lampshade.
Suggested lampbase height: 8″.

PLATE 31

Design 46
For a 10-sided lampshade.
Suggested lampbase height: 6″.

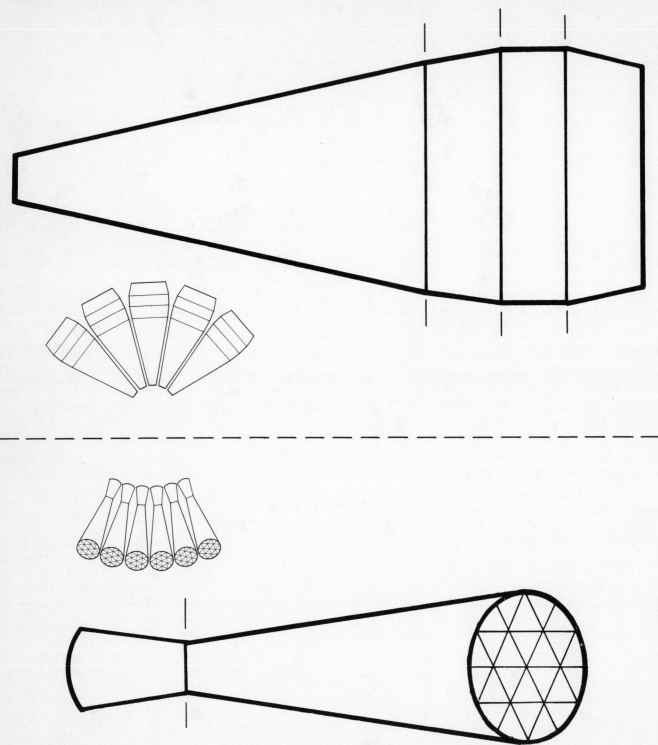

Design 47
For a 12-sided lampshade.
Suggested lampbase height: 6″.

PLATE 32